Jesus walks on the water

urban spirit!
inspire higher

After Jesus had fed the five thousand, his disciples got into a boat to cross over the lake to Bethsaida. Jesus stayed there to tell the people they could go home. Then he told them goodbye and went up on the side of a mountain to pray.

Later that same evening, Jesus was still on the mountain alone.

By this time, the boat was already far away
somewhere in the middle of the lake.

The boat was having trouble because of the waves, and the wind was blowing against it. The disciples were struggling very hard to keep control of the boat against the strong winds.

Between three and six o'clock in the morning, Jesus' followers were still in the boat. Jesus came to them. He was walking on the water. When the followers saw him walking on the water, they were afraid. They said, "It's a ghost!" and cried out in fear.

But Jesus quickly spoke to them.
He said, have courage! It is I! Don't be afraid."

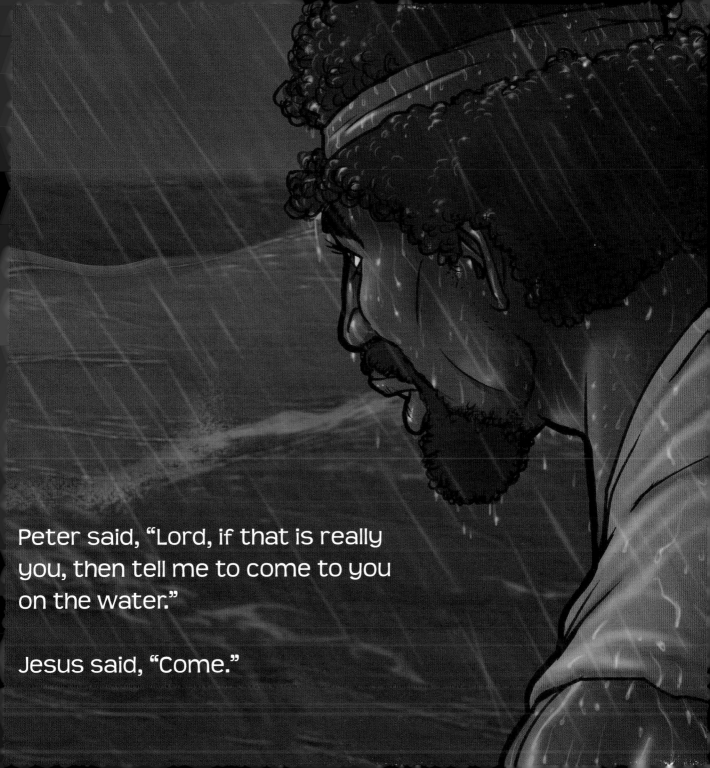

Peter said, "Lord, if that is really you, then tell me to come to you on the water."

Jesus said, "Come."

And Peter left the boat and walked on the water to Jesus.

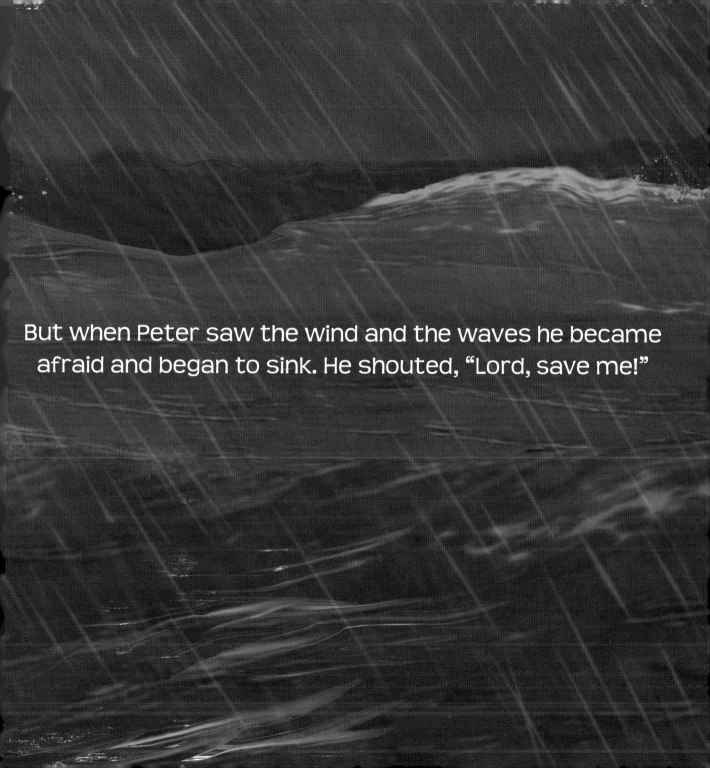

But when Peter saw the wind and the waves he became afraid and began to sink. He shouted, "Lord, save me!"

Then Jesus reached out his hand and caught Peter.

Jesus said, "Your faith is small. Why did you doubt?"

After Peter and Jesus were in the boat, the wind became calm. Then those who were in the boat worshiped Jesus and said, "Truly you are the Son of God!"

After they crossed the lake, they came to the shore of Gennesaret. As soon as they got out of the boat, the people recognized Jesus.

The next day came. Some people had stayed on the other side of the lake. They knew that Jesus had not gone in the boat with his followers but that they had left without him. And they knew that only one boat had been there. But then some boats came from Tiberias.

They landed near the place where the people had eaten the bread after the Lord had given thanks. The people saw that Jesus and his followers were not there now. So they got into their boats and went to Capernaum. They wanted to find Jesus.

The People found Jesus on the other side of the lake. They asked him, "Teacher, when did you come here?"

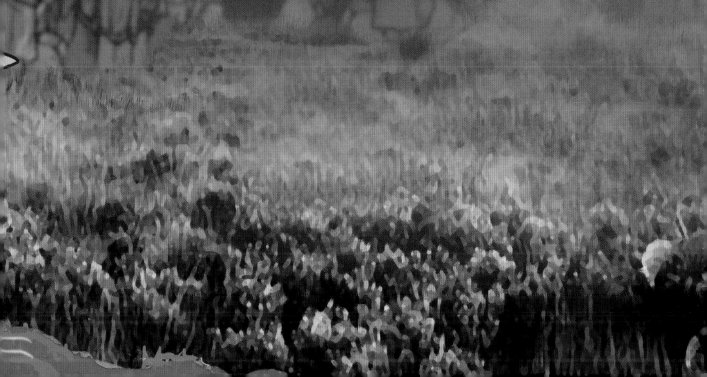

Jesus answered, "Are you looking for me because you saw me do miracles? No! I tell you the truth. You are looking for me because you ate the bread and were satisfied. Earthly food spoils and ruins. So don't work to get that kind of food. But work to get the food that stays good always and gives you eternal life. The Son of Man will give you that food. God the Father has shown that he is with the Son of man."

The people said, "Sir, give us this bread always."

Then Jesus said, "I am the bread that gives life. He who comes to me will never be hungry. He who believes in me will never be thirsty. But as I told you before, you have seen me, and still you don't believe. The father gives me my people. Every one of them will come to me and I will always accept them."

But the people still came to Jesus, not to believe in him as the Son of God, but so that he could heal them and perform other miracles. So they ran all over that part of the country to bring their sick people to him. They brought them each time they heard where he was. In every village or farm or marketplace where Jesus went, the people brought their sick to him.

They begged him to let them just touch his clothes, and everyone who did was healed.

Taken from: Matthew 14:22-26; John 6:22-27, 34-37

SHARE TIMELESS BIBLE STORIES
AND BIBLICAL TRUTHS AND MAKE READING THE BIBLE WITH YOUR FAMILY INTERESTING AND FUN!

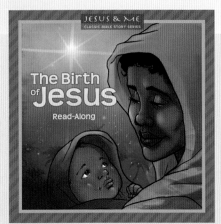

ISBN 978-0-9638127-5-9

ISBN 978-0-9638127-2-8

ISBN 978-0-9638127-7-3

PERFECT FOR SICK DAYS, VACATION DAYS, AUTO TRIPS AND GIFT GIVING THROUGHOUT THE YEAR.

Also available with an Audio CD containing:

❯ Word for word narration to help build vocabulary and encourage independent reading
❯ Clear concise narration with vivid sound effects
❯ Bonus Stories and Bonus Music included on CD